Amazing Grace

JOHN NEWTON

ARTWORK *by* GRAEME HEWITSON

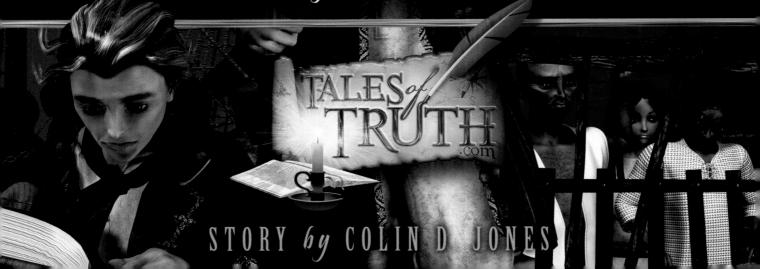

TALES *of* TRUTH
.com

STORY *by* COLIN D JONES

© Day One Publications 2016
First printed 2016

ISBN 9781846255212

Published by Day One Publications
Ryelands Road, Leominster, HR6 8NZ
TEL 01568 613 740 FAX 01568 611 473
Email: sales@dayone.co.uk
Website: www.dayone.co.uk

Cover design and illustrations by Graeme Hewitson
Internal design and typesetting by Dave Hewer

Printed by Orchard Press Cheltenham Ltd

To my young grandchildren; Naomi, Joshua, Isaac and Hannah, who like all children, were born slaves to sin (Romans 6:17). My earnest prayer for them and for every child reading this book, is they be set free from sin and become slaves of righteousness (Romans 6:18). It is the path the amazing grace of God allowed John Newton to walk.

Colin

Dedicated to the countless slaves throughout history who lived without freedom, and to the memory of John Newton who found freedom in Christ.

Graeme

JOHN NEWTON
AMAZING GRACE

John loved his mother so much; she was kind and gentle so different from his father. He was a ship's captain and could be very strict indeed. Secretly, John was glad that he was often away at sea. Every Sunday John would go with his mother to a church called the 'Independent Meeting Hall' where the preacher would talk about the Lord Jesus Christ.

One day his mother set out to visit some really good friends called the Cattlett family. He happily waved goodbye as the carriage pulled away from their home. He wished he could go with her but didn't mind too much as in just two weeks it would be his seventh birthday and he was sure she would never miss that.

He had no idea that his mother was very, very ill and that he would never see her again.

 9

Very soon after his mother's death his father married again. His stepmother wasn't cruel like the ones you read about in stories, but she didn't love John and he felt very lost and alone. The visits to church stopped and John began to forget the lessons he had learnt there.

John began to live two lives. In front of his father and stepmother he was well behaved and polite but as soon as he was out of their sight he would change. He made bad friends and got into all kinds of naughty ways. More times than he could remember his father punished him for some misbehaviour or another.

Sad and sullen, he knew he was not the young man his Christian mother would have wanted him to be.

More than once things happened that made him promise himself that he would change. When he was twelve he was thrown from a horse. He nearly landed on a sharp fence stake. He realised how close he had been to death and it frightened him. He made up his mind to start living a better life, but he soon forgot.

John was always late. One day he had agreed to meet a friend so that they could take a rowing boat out to a ship in the harbour. As usual John lost track of time and was annoyed to find that his friend had left without him. He was cross, not with himself for being late but with his friend for going without him.

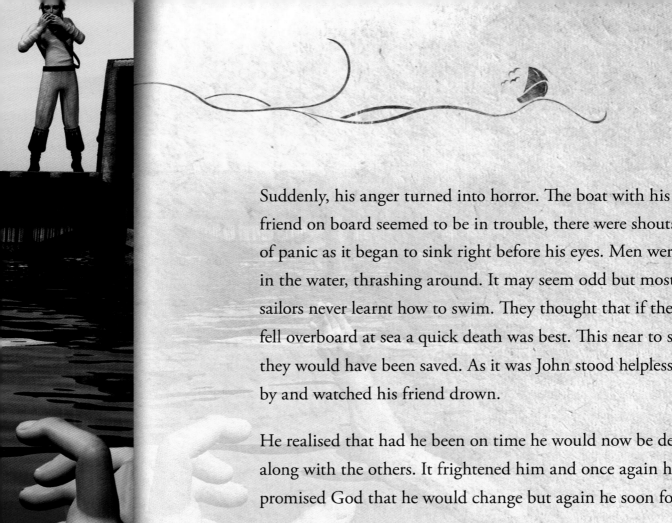

Suddenly, his anger turned into horror. The boat with his friend on board seemed to be in trouble, there were shouts of panic as it began to sink right before his eyes. Men were in the water, thrashing around. It may seem odd but most sailors never learnt how to swim. They thought that if they fell overboard at sea a quick death was best. This near to shore they would have been saved. As it was John stood helplessly by and watched his friend drown.

He realised that had he been on time he would now be dead along with the others. It frightened him and once again he promised God that he would change but again he soon forgot.

In 1742 John now seventeen received a letter that was to change his life. The Catlett family invited him for Christmas. Mr and Mrs Catlett had six children, but as far as John was concerned there was only one person that mattered. Their daughter Mary (though everyone called her Polly) was 14 and John immediately fell in love with her.

Many years later he said that he had loved her at first sight and never ceased to love her for a single moment. Theirs was the love that stories are written about.

He was supposed to stay three days but made the visit last three weeks. In doing so, he missed a ship to the West Indies where his father had found work for him.

As John expected, his father was very angry with him.

The Navy in those days was a cruel place to earn a living. Sailors were treated very badly so few ever volunteered to join up. Instead, men were 'pressed' which often meant knocked on the head in some tavern only to wake up at sea and part of the crew of some ship.

John idling around the docks one day was suddenly 'pressed' into the crew of HMS Harwich. Even his father felt sorry for him and while he could not get him released he did get him promoted to Midshipman the lowest officer rank. John used his improved situation, not to better himself, but instead he became a bully to the sailors under him.

John was granted a days leave which he used to visit the Catletts again. Mr Catllett did not approve of his love for Mary. They were, he said, both too young and that John showed no signs of ever being able to make a good living for himself let alone a wife. John saddened by this was late back to his ship much to the Captains anger.

It was then he made the most stupid decision of his life. Lovesick and desperately unhappy he left his ship without permission. This was called desertion and was a very serious crime indeed. In his mind he would walk to see Mary then plead with his father to get him released from the Navy.

Once again the whole course of his life was to change for the worse.

John looked every inch the sailor so he was soon arrested by some soldiers called Dragoons and dragged back to *HMS Harwich* under arrest. The anger in the Captain's face convinced him that he would receive no mercy. The verdict was that John was to be flogged. He was tied up and as the rest of the crew watched on silently, he was beaten by a sailor known as the Master at Arms.

We don't know how many times John was hit, but it was the worst pain he would ever know in his life.

When the flogging was over he was carried below deck to spend painful days and nights recovering. As he lay there he wanted only two things, to kill the Captain and then to die himself. He seriously thought of throwing himself overboard to drown.

As further punishment he was stripped of his rank and was now at the mercy of those he had bullied.

Only the thought of Mary stopped him carrying out either wish. John was sinking lower and lower into sin. He drank whenever he could and became very unpopular with both the officers and the crew. It was at this time that his life changed once again.

Navy ships had the power to stop merchant ships and force them to exchange good sailors for bad ones. When *HMS Harwich* met the *Pegasus* at sea, John, realising that this was a chance to escape the Navy, pleaded with the Captain to transfer him. He only agreed because his other officers supported the request. They did so not out of kindness but because they wanted to get rid of a troublesome and useless sailor.

So John exchanged life in the Navy for that in the slave trade.

Sierra Leone

The slave trade was a terrible thing. Men women and children were captured in Africa and became part of what was known as the 'Triangle Trade'. Ships set sail from England to Africa with a cargo that was used to buy the slaves. They were then taken to America and the West Indies to be sold as slave workers. The money gained bought spices which were then taken back to England. The country was growing rich on this human misery. John was now a part of it.

Before they could be shipped they were held in terrible conditions. White men like John had no resistance to the diseases in Africa and many of the sailors as well as the slaves died in this shameful trade.

The Captain of the *Pegasus* died of disease shortly after John joined the ship. The man that took his place was no friend of John's so when the opportunity came John left the ship to work for a Mr Clow. He was now in charge of the slaves on land. John did not realise that Clow was a cheat who would never pay him any wages. To add to his misery the owners of the *Pegasus* lost all their money so there was no pay from them either. He was alone, without money and stranded in Africa far away from home.

He lived little better than the slaves themselves, sleeping where and when he could and eating whatever scraps he could find. He thought he could not be more miserable and longed for Mary and for home.

It was only a matter of time before he caught the African Fever from which few recovered.

Days and nights were spent in terrible agony, he had one nightmare after another reliving all the saddest moments of his life, his Mother's death, his Father's anger, his flogging. All were remembered again and again.

God had not forgotten John Newton and despite all his wicked ways God was working in his life because he had a great plan for this foolish young man.

So it was that the slaves began to pity him and do what little they could for him.

Slowly, a miracle began, the nightmares stopped and he started to dream of Mary. He was about to surprise everyone and recover. Yet he still did not turn to God but began to worship the African idols.

Once again his life was to change The Greyhound was sighted off shore, her Captain Joseph Manesty was a friend of John's father. His father had never stopped looking for John and had asked all his fellow Captains to keep an eye out for him. So it was that John again set sail for England. It was a long and difficult journey 7,000 sea miles going home past Cape Town, Brazil and Newfoundland.

John had little to do so the Captain lent him an Old book by Thomas àKempis called "The Imitation of Christ".

On March 10th 1748 The Greyhound entered a terrible storm. The sailors were used to storms but this one frightened even the most experienced of them with its power. Many were sure that they would sink.

There was a brief moment of hope when the storm died down and hasty repairs were made. John, afraid of death, took the opportunity to read from a book of sermons belonging to the Captain.

The truths he had learned in church with his mother came flooding back. He realised that he was a sinner and that unless he accepted what Jesus had done on the Cross he would be lost forever. It was the first time in his life he knew that he must turn to Christ to be saved.

Soon however, hope was dashed and the storm returned with even greater force. For four weeks the ship was driven onwards in utter darkness. Several members of the crew died. Then suddenly, it was over and the crippled ship struggled into port in the North of Ireland

Once the danger was over, most of the sailors returned to their old ways. Some of them had blamed the storm on John saying he was like Jonah and had brought disaster on them because of his sins. They were now in the taverns sinning as much as they could.

John however, was truly a changed man. What he could never do by simply saying he would change had happened because God had saved him and he was now a Christian. Instead of Taverns he was to be found in Church eager to learn more about Christ.

He pledged to God that he would never again live as he had been living but to live for Christ. It was a promise that God by his grace helped him to keep till the day he died.

John was now a very different man. He looked for his father to say how sorry he was but he had already left to take up a post as Governor of Hudson Bay. John had to be content to write and say sorry.

He turned down a job as Captain choosing instead to be the First Mate on *The Brownlow*.

His other great desire was to see his beloved Mary. So he wrote a very humble letter confessing all his many faults and begging her father for permission to visit. Permission was not granted for him to visit but he was allowed to write to her.

Having spent all his money looking for his father and unwilling to be in debt he walked from Chatham in Kent to Liverpool to join his new ship.

John was still involved in the slave trade, which we might find hard to understand. Sometimes, Christians learn very slowly what is right and what is wrong. Sometimes, they say and do things that they really shouldn't. God was still at work in John's life and he still had much to learn. The temptations on board a ship were great and he did not live a blameless life but he never returned to his old ways.

One thing he had learned was wrong was what the Bible calls blasphemy. That is using God's name in a wrong way. Later in life he would refer to himself as the "Old Blasphemer". That was one sin he never committed again.

Slowly, he was changing and soon he was ready to Captain his own ship.

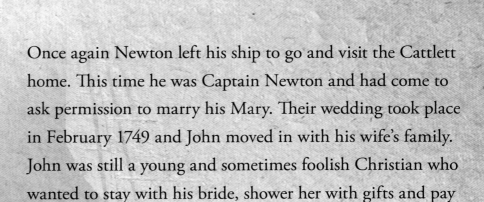

Once again Newton left his ship to go and visit the Cattlett home. This time he was Captain Newton and had come to ask permission to marry his Mary. Their wedding took place in February 1749 and John moved in with his wife's family. John was still a young and sometimes foolish Christian who wanted to stay with his bride, shower her with gifts and pay off his debts.

The only way he could see to do this was to win the lottery so he wasted what little money he had on lottery tickets.

God saw to it that he did not win a single penny. So soon after their marriage he was forced to set sail again.

As a Captain he held regular services for the crew and tried to ease the suffering of the slaves.

A collapse and ill health ended his career at sea and he became the 'Customs and Excise Officer" at Liverpool. He began to study the Bible in Hebrew and in Greek. He spoke with many of the great Christian men of his day including George Whitfield and Henry Venn. In 1758 he preached his first sermon, which was a disaster and ended with the Pastor preaching his text for him.

Undeterred he continued to study and also to write and again to preach. He was beginning to feel the call of God to the Christian Ministry.

He published an account of his life and conversion called "an Authentic Narrative" that was so well received, that eventually, he was offered a position as curate at St Peter and St Paul in Olney Buckinghamshire.

John and Mary had moved to one of the poorest towns in England. John's great friend the hymn writer William Cowper called them "half starved and ragged". They lived as cheaply as possible in order to help these poor people in every way they could. They often fed people after the morning service who were too poor to feed themselves.

John loved these poor people and they soon grew to love him. He longed for them to know Christ as he did and never missed an opportunity to speak to them. Again and again he would tell his story of God's amazing grace in his life.

All hours of the day and night, John was a well known sight in his old sea coat visiting from home to home.

John was never a great preacher. In his day sermons often lasted for as long as two hours. His were always described as short. What he was very good at, was knowing the needs of his people and preaching in a way that helped them. He often gave colourful illustrations from his life experience.

He started Prayer Meetings, arranged lunches for those who had walked more than six miles to church, had children's and young people's Bible Studies and also time for those interested in the faith to ask questions.

People came to hear him from further and further away. They came in the rain and in the snow and many came to know Christ as their Saviour and Lord.

Olney had never known such a time of blessing

Amazing Grace
Amazing Grace, How Sweet the Sound,
That saved a wretch like me
I once was Lost but now am Found,
Was Blind, but now, I see.

His work was not confined to Olney, he was often invited to speak in other churches and in the homes of rich and influential people. He always spoke about Christ but also was very active in raising money for the poor and needy.

He was a great letter writer, many of which were later collected and published.

He is also well known as a hymn writer. He and William Cowper together wrote a hymn Book for their own church called *The Olney Hymns* which is still in print today.

His best know hymn by far is *Amazing Grace*. Based on his own experience of God, it has become a firm favourite with Christians everywhere. A version of it with bagpipes even topped the pop music charts around the world in 1972.

One last great change was to happen in John's life, in 1779 he left Olney for St Mary's Church Woolnoth in London. It was there that he met the troubled MP for Hull, William Wilberforce.

William declared that John was the means under God of bringing him to a firm faith in Christ.

Wilberforce devoted 44 years of his life to one great end, the evil Slave Trade. John was to be a great ally in this fight. Who better than one who both engaged in the trade and been little better than a slave himself to speak of its evils. John published his *Thoughts on the African Slave Trade* in 1788. Throughout the fight William and John stood together. It was a fight that was only finally won in 1807 the year both men died.

In 1790 after a long illness Mary died of cancer. In those last years he spent every moment he could with the woman he still said he adored. On one occasion he was heard to say, "The world seemed to die with her". Many wondered if he would survive, even whether his faith could survive this tragedy.

The answer was clear when the next Sunday he preached powerfully from a text in Habakkuk 3:17–18:

Though the fig tree should not blossom,
nor fruit be on the vines,
the produce of the olive fail
and the fields yield no food,
the flock be cut off from the fold
and there be no herd in the stalls,
yet I will rejoice in the LORD;
I will take joy in the God of my salvation.

JOHN NEWTON
DIED 21ST DECR 1807
AGED 82

MARY NEWTON
DIED 15TH DECR 1790
AGED 61

John outlived Mary by 17 years, at the age of 76 he was still preaching. Well into his 80's he was being sought out by people for spiritual advice and counsel. In an age obsessed with last words he once said "tell me not how a man died but how he lived".

All are agreed John Newton lived because of "Amazing Grace". The "Old Blasphemer" died peacefully in Christ having helped stop the Slave Trade he once served.

He was buried in Olney and wrote the words to be placed on his own gravestone:

John Newton
Clerk
Once An Infidel And Libertine
A Servant Of Slaves In Africa
Was By The Rich Mercy Of Our Lord And Saviour Jesus Christ
Preserved, Restored, Pardoned
And Appointed To Preach Faith

THE
END

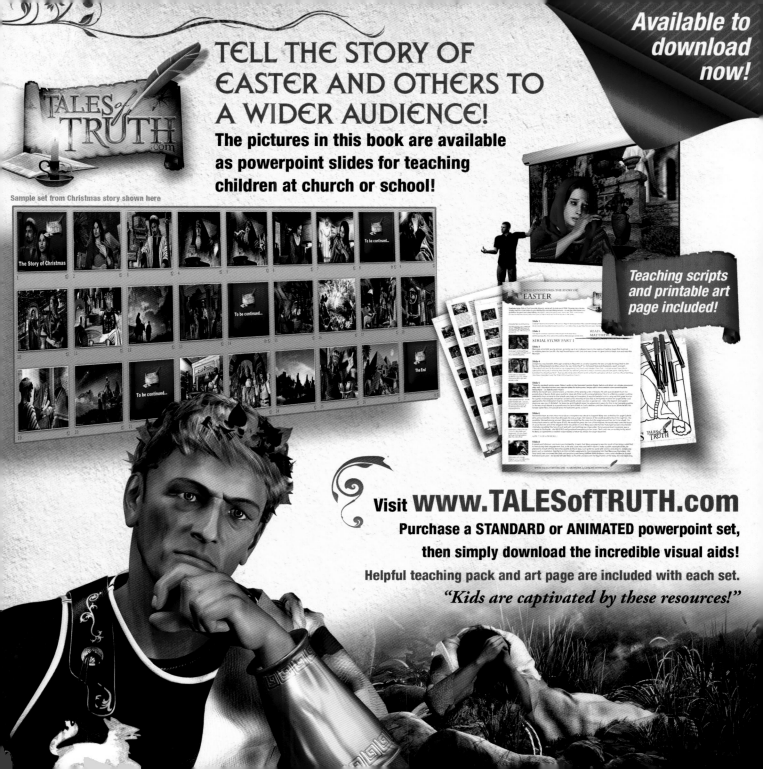